The Art of Living Dangerously

————— ❧❦❧ —————

The rebels guide to thriving in a world that expects you to conform

Jennifer Murphy

Table of Contents

Acknowledgements

This book is dedicated to my son, Alexander Lewis. Every single day he inspires me to live dangerously, to live life on my terms. He is an amazing old soul who is already thriving on his own path in this crazy world that keeps asking for him to conform. You are the most important being in the world squeak and I love you. Play your game son, play your game.

I must thank my partner Craig for his encouragement and certain belief I can do anything I set my mind to achieve.

To my parents, Mark and Cindy for always letting me be me and trusting me to be okay. I know spirit sent me to the right people for this lifetime.

And to Patrick and Marie Dahdal for being there when I needed the push to get this book out there. Timing is everything.

Introduction

White Sheets

Wwhat could white sheets possibly have to do with rebelling? I mean aren't white sheets about as boring as you can get, as normal as you can get...maybe even as expected as you can get?

Not really. It's harder than you think to find crisp white, high quality plain white sheets. Everyone wants to add a pattern or make them "fancy" somehow. As if simple is somehow not good enough.

Regardless, white sheets became important to me when I received an honest look at the life I really wanted to be living instead of the one I was.

In 2004, I left a successful military career. I had served for over 7 years active duty and decided to transition to the reserves, then national guard upon completion of my service for a total of 10 years. During my time in the Army I deployed twice taking on surreal tasks like establishing logistics supply lines for the Afghanistan Operation and being the White House Liaison for the US President's first trip to the Middle East after we decided to go to war with Iraq (again). I had been awarded a bronze star and was being offered opportunities to work with elite Army units. I wanted more – I wanted to thrive though I didn't yet have that word.

I had grown up without much in terms of material wealth. I knew my family loved me, there was never an issue there, but I saw things and experiences my peers were having, both real and imagined, and I wanted those things and experiences too. It reached its pinnacle, or maybe the rock bottom, depending on how you look at it, when my father was in a horrible accident the year I turned 13.

I had just started high school and was home alone on a Friday afternoon. My mom was working the closing shift at her job as a grocery store manager. My dad was due home from work late afternoon and would pick up my much younger brothers on his way. As it grew darker I began to worry, amplified due to lack of electricity or phone. My dad was supposed to have paid our electric and phone on his way home since both had been cut off. Neither was on and I was alone without a way to contact anyone or light the house. Just after dark I was mustering the courage to go to the neighbors for help when lights hit the front window.

I was so relieved until I saw it was my brother's babysitter. She explained my mother had been taken to the city nearest our small mountain town to be with my father as he had been in a minor accident. I intuitively knew there was more to it. There was.

My father had rolled his truck several times and been thrown out somewhere along the way. He had a severe head injury, multiple stitch-worthy lacerations and was in and out of coherent consciousness. On a lighter note, my dad is a pretty funny guy and they couldn't exactly tell when he was kidding and what was head trauma.... we still wonder sometimes.

The punchline is within 12 months we had lost our home to the bank and were living on the goodwill of a loving neighbor in a house that had seen better times. My mother struggled to keep us afloat on her grocery store job and we somehow survived.

That time in my life cemented so many of the things I had already seen: my parents struggling to keep the three of us in clothes and food, not having a phone or electricity, our wood supply which brought us heat in the mountain winters barely keeping up, my parents frustration at the entire situation and the fights it sometimes caused.

I vowed I'd live better. Better translated to different. I ran as fast and as far as I could for different.

I tried a lot of things I thought would be the solution. Some would be not so healthy: men and alcohol mostly. Others were not horrible: college, a full ROTC scholarship, working two jobs. I married a man who was on paper awesome, but together we were a disaster. We divorced after 18 months – while I was on my first combat deployment. Sometimes we must fight on multiple fronts. In total, I tried and tested as many things as I could and I pursued a success I perceived would make me feel happy, satisfied and fulfilled. I still wasn't thriving.

As I left my successful US Army career as a captain, I wasn't sure where to go or what to do. A job fair in Washington DC led me to a job in Cedar Rapids, Iowa as the first female maintenance manager in a power plant for a large Midwest utility company. It was a direct translation of my skills earned in the Army as a logistician and it was for a big company. Seemed like success. I realized later it was conformity.

I bought a house I didn't need: a four-bedroom 2.5 bath with a white picket fence in suburbia where my two labs could run around in the yard and jump the fence if they really wanted to – which they did. My neighbors were all family people so I got a family. I married my son's father who already had two boys entering their teen years.

I changed jobs not too much later and found myself working for a large defense contractor working long hours in the office and longer out of it. I got pregnant with the son I had so desperately wanted and he, being my child, decided he didn't want to wait the full 9 months to arrive and joined us 3 months prematurely.

It was then I had to take stock.

I had spent 3 weeks in the hospital on bed rest before he arrived, giving me plenty of alone time to think. My son's father was starting a new job and had a life he wanted to keep living. My time in the hospital was focused on keeping my son in the womb, staying positive and being as healthy as I could be. I also looked to the future.

I began the process of thinking about the life I wanted to live. No one had ever asked me what I wanted out of life. I had been given choices about classes to take in school, clothes to wear, men to date, books to read, trips to take...but the big picture was never really explored.

I hadn't ever really explored it myself. I had been so focused on getting to the next milestone, or the next decision or moving so fast away from something, I didn't slow down enough to see where I was in time and space. I most certainly didn't pay attention to anything longer term – other than what everyone else seemed to be plodding toward. I had traded my desire to thrive for conformity – without conscious thought.

In this time of being confined and unable to go anywhere, I explored. I realized I wasn't truly happy. And I felt guilty about it. I intellectually understood this was complete bullshit, but the guilt persisted, so I shoved it down.

I took my son home, we began our life and it soon became a war zone at my house. Very little I did felt good enough. The war wasn't always external, sometimes it was just within me. Arguments rooted in dissatisfaction cropped up regularly and time and again I ignored the neon flashing sign in my mind's eye: "change is needed".

On a trip to Australia for work I received an email from a close friend. She shared with me a woman she admired was coming to town to do some one on one work and advised me to book a session. I called from Australia to the place she'd be and made sure I got some time reserved. My soul wouldn't let me sleep until I did – it knew this was going to spark the change it had been flashing.

She told me everything I already knew but was afraid to voice. It was exhilarating and terrifying all at once. Here is where I tried to defeat myself.

I was making over six figures in income. My spouse made a bit less, but together we approached $200,000 a year with our investments and income. I told her I was too broke to pay the $650 needed for a coaching program. I felt broke. We had created a lifestyle that had us living paycheck to paycheck with houses, cars, trips, luxuries and the miscellaneous crap "needed" to maintain.... I don't even know what.

She offered a "love donation" option and I took it. I began working with her and today I can say, when, I strike it rich, she will never want for anything. It changed my life.

For the first time, I felt like someone was asking me what I wanted and truly listening. I was being given space to explore what was authentic for me. I started with the idea that I simply needed a new job and I'd be happy. Her response was to ask me how my marriage was. It took me a while to understand we are not box living creatures. What is happening in one area of our lives is intertwined with all the other areas. If works sucks, family life is tougher – and it flows both ways.

She had me look at what my ideal life was, over and over and each time I would get more clarity. Then she challenged me to find one thing in my ideal I could act on immediately. My answer was white sheets.

In my vision, I woke up every day in crisp white cotton sheets with a fresh breeze blowing through the window. My room was simple, clutter free and airy. I was refreshed and happy to be me.

Introduction - White Sheets

I bought the sheets – in fact I found an amazing online deal and bought 2 sets!

No one in my life understood why I wanted change: I was making good money, had a nice suburban house, drove a current year SUV, had a husband, good kids, seemed to know enough people and was busy with volunteer work. From the outside, I was living the dream.

On the inside, I was feeling trapped, smothered and completely empty. Guilt struck when I admitted the only thing I didn't want to let go of in my life was my son. Guilt pounded me hard. How dare I have created all of this "success" and only want my son from it? I stayed where I was longer because of guilt.

Those white sheets were the ignition for the rebellion that had sparked long ago. They set me on the path to become free of the guilt, to rebel against what everyone else thought I "should" be happy with and to allow myself to create a life I can wake up loving.

We deserve this. We get only so many trips around the sun in this lifetime. I can't believe we are supposed to settle. I believe we are supposed to push boundaries, test limits and see what we can achieve with the full spectrum of our energies. We have them for a reason – it's not to put them on a shelf and admire the dust they collect. There isn't a right way to exercise them, but we must. We must rebel against the idea that we shouldn't.

It's time to create your own rebellion. It's time to live dangerously and embrace what your soul is asking YOU for.

Mine asked me to embrace independence, freedom and the path of transformation – starting with white sheets.

What will your white sheets be?

Take some time now to open yourself up to the voice within you. Close your eyes and just breathe. When you ask, what do I really want? What does your soul answer?

Five Things to Do Now to Answer this Question:

1. Spend 15 minutes writing about what you'd do if you won $50 million tomorrow. Yep, I know you'd give a butt-load to charity and pay off bills and buy your gramma a house...but then what?

2. Make a list of who you admire most and why. What do they do that is so awesome? They are a mirror of your own qualities. Those things you love most about them are within you – write them all down then say them all as "I am" statements.

3. What advice would you give 10-year-old you? How can you take it now? If you think 10-year-old you should join the sports team you didn't join...why don't you go join a sports team? We think we have missed opportunities when really, we haven't. They just shifted on our timeline.

4. Finish this sentence as many times as you can in 5 minutes: "If only I could...." This prompt is the gateway to the wishes of our soul. With every completed statement, you throw a coin in the spiritual wishing

well. Now pick one to try. A wish is fabulous, but picking one to act on is even better.

5. Make a list of all the things you LOVE about you. You must, (yes must), love yourself enough to push through this transformation. Love is the force behind it all. It makes zero sense to hate yourself and carry hate through to a new life – you won't create your ideal life, you'll create some new version of hell for yourself. This rebellion is about change for awesomeness. You can't be awesome if you won't let love in. Go ahead, tell you how much you love you and all the ways you do. Love.

Chapter 1:

The Birth of Rebellion

How does one arrive at the point of needing to rebel against every self and externally imposed limitation wrought upon them?

The clues lie in a few areas and can be persistent in only one, or all of them. In fact, we may believe them to persist in only one, yet as we investigate, we will quickly realize roots have spread to all areas of our life.

We are not silo beings.

We do not exist in one silo, work for example, and switch silos, isolating from the previous with no connection. We are more like big vats of multi-ingredient soup; all those flavors in there mixing and simmering together.

The areas I'll talk about here are the heaviest hitters - the more obvious areas where people are likely to find symptoms at the surface level where they are ready to be seen.

Health.

If your health is not optimal, you know it. You know if you have extra weight, chronic illness or stress induced pain. You know it. You also know it is in your control. If you are not eating the highest quality food available to you and getting at least 20 minutes of physical activity a day you aren't even trying. And drink some water for goodness sake. There is no reason not to take care of the one body you get for this lifetime.

If you choose not to, you are damaging every other area: increased sick days from work, missed family events, increased financial burden, missing fun with friends and not caring for you.

This was the second area I tackled in my big change after the white sheets. I transitioned slowly to organic animal products, then vegetables, then cut out all remaining processed foods and eliminated soda. I lost weight, saved money on food since I didn't need as much as what I was buying and eating was so much higher quality, and am sick only 1-2 times a year instead of 1-2 times a week.

So how is your health?

Career Satisfaction.

If you hate your job, it will bleed in to all the other areas of your life. This is common sense. You spend a lot of hours at work. When you don't like your job, you then tend to think about how much you don't like it everywhere else you go. It adds stress and you get ill, or you miss work and lose money. Your friends don't want to hang because all you do is bitch about your boss or co-worker and you can't relax enough to enjoy your personal time.

I came home from work nightly and spent at least 45 minutes railing about my job. Then I began to get right in other areas and could find more right in my work. As I found more right in my work, more of everything else seemed more right. Opportunity opened, I changed jobs, then took the opportunity to leap into entrepreneurship. A career hating person carries hate with them. A career okay person can translate much more easily into high energy creating.

In love with your career?

Money.

Your stress goes way up when you can't meet basic needs. It also goes up when you perceive you aren't keeping up with your perceived peer group. I say perceived because you have chosen to try to keep up. You can say no to this.

If you don't have your bank account balanced, don't have your bills on a schedule and don't know what is going out or coming in, it will impact every other area of your life. Cancelled nights out, resentment about your salary at work, stress in the family and no money for self-care can get old real fast.

Remember when I talked about being broke even though I was making multiple 6 figures? That was a choice. I chose to immerse in that feeling. I chose to create a lifestyle that had me dependent on my job, instead of letting my job support my lifestyle. The second is optimal. The first is gross in my book.

Finger on the pulse of where your money is going in and out?

Relationships.

The people closest to you tend to bear the burden when anything bad is happening around you. They also benefit from the celebrations. When you are thriving in all areas of your life, your relationships will also thrive. People will want to be around you and you will love being around them.

I'll talk more about who to surround yourself with later. Here I will say, pay attention to who you have around you. Healthy relationships breed healthy you and unhealthy relationships breed unhealthy you – no matter what is happening everywhere else.

Who do you need to let go of and who do you need to touch base with?

Self-Care.

How well do you prioritize you? I know I am a mess if I don't get some me time periodically. I must. I must get me time. It doesn't have to be expensive me time and this is where some people get caught up sometimes. They can't afford the treatment they want to, they skip it. How about finding an alternative?

Or worse, they won't spend money they do possess, instead spending it on everyone else around them: friends, kids, spouses, co-workers even. They may be hoping someone will return the favor or looking for the pat on the back that says they are awesome. But if you just keep giving without refilling you...where does it keep coming from?

Taking time to be with just you in this crazy busy world allows you to get in touch with what matters most to you. Otherwise, all you hear is everyone else telling you what should be important to you. Should is a four-letter word here. No "shoulding" allowed when it comes to self-care. Only wanting and being.

How will you care for you this week?

Social Life.

Yes, you are entitled to a social life and it isn't dependent on what everyone else is doing or wants to do. If no one you know wants to do what you want to do, go do it anyway and meet someone there. Trust me, there are people out there who dig the same kind of shit you do.

My ex-husband loved to go see local bands live at local bars. I like live music, but I wasn't a big fan of the bar scene or most of the people there. Not my crowd. I didn't go after a few times of trying to make it work. He could go, I just wouldn't go with – I don't get to tell others what is okay for them. We were both happier if I got to go do my thing or stay home and do my thing.

What is on your social agenda this month?

A few other things to ignite rebellion around:

Finding "work life balance".

That phrase makes me seriously want to gag. I am so sick of hearing people toss this phrase around as if it means something. It doesn't. It's a pretty label for being continuously under the gun to "measure up" "meet expectations" and toe the line someone else drew.

So, if you are seeking work life balance – stop now. Stop it. Banish the word from your vocabulary and pull that thought out of your head now. It's a bullshit cover up, a half measure to what you really want. Instead, seek rebellion against living someone else's idea of okay.

Someday Syndrome

Also known as living for retirement. I'm done hearing people talk about what they will do someday. I'm over living for some mythical future. You have now. Do it now, live it now, experience it now. Now is a fabulous place to exist, be in it.

Not in some bullshit existential spouting off platitudes kind of way, but in a dirt under your fingernails, sweat streaming down your ass crack digging deep kind of way. Every moment is a god damn gift. Act like it – live the life you have right in front of you. Talk to the people across the table from you. Hug your parents. Fuck someday. Go live your life now.

Living for your Kids.

Yep, parents I am talking to you. Your kids get their own life and so do you. Yep, love the living shit out of them. They are awesome. I love my son more than the air I breathe. He is an amazing being whom I adore having in my world. But he isn't my reason for being. (insert collective GASP.) He isn't. I am my reason for being. His existence makes being me a better experience.

He gets to choose his experiences and I get to choose mine. Last year I took a trip without him and oh my lord did he try like heck to worm his way into my guilt center to push the buttons. He cried and whined and told me how terrible the camp he was going to while I was gone was and how boring his dad was and how I was mean for leaving him behind.

I had braced for it though. I was ready for his attack. Did I miss him? Hell yes. Did I allow myself to wallow in guilt for leaving him behind? Hell no. I told him I loved him and was looking forward to seeing him and I hung up. Then we went and did some lampworking, explored outdoor stores and sampled shops in Colorado.

Stop doing what everyone else is doing. Especially if the pants don't fit.

I love to watch people. I watch them a lot. We are funny – sometimes hilariously, sometimes tragically. Fashion is the biggest following I see going tragic quickly. I realize I am opening myself up for "stop body shaming women!" kinds of comments and I am not attempting to be judgmental when I say this.... sometimes the shorts weren't made for you.

They look awful, you look awful and I can tell you are incredibly uncomfortable by the way you keep tugging them down out of your ass and squirming. Why are you wearing them?

If any article of clothing makes you feel like you must always be adjusting, pitch it. It isn't for you. You will never look like the confident man or woman you are trying to emulate. Find clothing that makes you feel comfortable without the workout.

And the same goes for ideas. Just because everyone is doing the meditation, reading the book, taking the class doesn't mean it's right for you. I have been unable to finish more than one book I simply "had to read!" according to people I know. "You'll love it!" they promised. Ummmm, no. I didn't. Oprah and I don't always agree on what is a fabulous book.

I didn't like Lean in, I wasn't a huge fan of the style of Eat, Pray, Love and I thought fifty shades of gray was more hilarious than sensual. Seriously... just because it is popular doesn't make it good. No more so than the ubiquitous annoying bitch in high school was the best life had to offer.

Fuck diets, start eating right and drinking water.

Why is there a health food aisle in the grocery store? Shouldn't it all be healthy?

The fact that we need to delineate this scares the hell out of me because most shoppers spend the bulk of their time outside the health food aisle. Before our neighborhood co-op moved to town, I adored shopping in the "health food" aisle because no one else was. I was all alone to peruse and choose and not have some mouth breather impatiently tapping their plastic flip flop behind me.

Know what you are putting into your body. Pay attention – your body will tell you what is working and what isn't. I talked about how your health is telling you how you need a rebellion earlier in this section. It's time to get informed. If you can't understand what is in that boxed product in your cart, how do you know it is good for you?

I like soups where I can tell you exactly what the ingredient list says. I enjoy bread where the ingredients are things like local organic wheat, sugar, butter, salt...not ethyl parathion. I know what wheat flour, sugar and butter is. I am not sure what ethyl parathion is exactly. And I definitely don't know what it is doing to my body. Why would I put it in there?

And water...it is more than 80% of your body and you "don't like it"??? You like coke and energy drinks better. Great. In the meantime, how's your weight? How is your skin? Pooping regularly? Any muscles soreness? Headaches? Yep, all signs of dehydration, not to mention who knows what the other crap is doing to you.

I cut out all processed, inorganic foods a few years ago. Today, if I try to eat any of it I am immediately sick. Immediately. I get a rash or a horrible stomach ache or both. My head will pound or I will feel nauseous. It is real and immediate.

Stop dieting. Start eating right and drinking water.

All these areas impact one another. A change in one will ripple into the others. A change in one can be the birthing point for your rebellion, the one that allows you to begin to live dangerously in the center of your souls calling. Allow the change to ripple.

Acknowledge that what you are shifting and beginning is the start of who you really are in this lifetime (and beyond).

These are all mindsets to approach. All ideas to incorporate at the levels right for you. Here are **5 ways to induce labor to birth your rebellion now:**

1. Identify where you see the similarities in the symptoms outlined above.

2. Acknowledge what you want to change.

3. Decide (powerful decision) to engage with rebellion.

4. Tell someone.

5. LOVE the ever-loving shit out of yourself enough to push through the pain of birth.

Chapter 2:

Igniting the Rebellion

Yaay! You've decided to make some changes. You are still reading. Sweet. Spirit is holding your rebellion baby by the ankles ready to swat its little ass to start the breathing.

You may be sensing some or all the following right now:

- Terror

- Anxiety

- Anticipation

- Excitement

- Exhilaration

- Love

- Hate

- Worry

- Guilt

- A sense of impending doom

- Immense Pride

- Restlessness

- A desire to drink, fuck or fight (or all three)

- Raw aggression

- Pure Ecstasy

All those emotions are perfectly natural. They are present because what you are about to undertake is real. Maybe for the first time in your life you are taking on something purely for you, your happiness and your sense of self. This is all on you, success or defeat, one way or another you are about to have an experience that will change some stuff in your world.

It's time to uncage the emotion and energy swirling within you. It's time to scream the scream, laugh the laugh, take what needs to be taken and ignite into.... your energy. No adjectives needed. It's time to ignite into your energy with all you have and all you are.

You defy adjectives. You defy description, you simply are you and you are worth igniting.

The energy within may feel like a nervous tingling at this stage, or perhaps a full-blown anxiety attack. The feeling is scary – the good kind. The kind you know will make you stronger and more awesome-r.

You feel like you are scrambling around, looking for something to root into, something to make it real. Something to ease the buildup and allow it to become the new normal.

It's time to take the first action. What is your white sheets? What is the thing you can do from that big vision you created you can do right now?

Choose it and begin.

To continue to make progress, get support. You are not an unsupported rebel.

It's time for a strike team.

Yes, rebellions ignite with one idea walking the border between madness and brilliance. They are fueled by fellow rebels and the resistance follows. They are fueled by the energy of others who come with them and even by those who attempt to naysay.

Your strike team is optimized when it is made from the ragtagest, gnarliest, orneriest, strong willed bunch of rebels and resistors you can find. Think of all the great rebellions – were they meek, weak willed subjects who cowered at loud noises? Nope. They were bad ass mofos who took the hills, sacked the castles and tore down all the shit in their way.

Do you need to go burn down your house, or your employer at this stage? No. In this day and age, it'll lead you to the opposite of what you are looking for: you'll find more bars than less and the independence you seek will be blocked by the cage you have created in a brand-new form.

What you do need are people who embody energy of a magnitude so great it pushes you higher: the fearless to speak their minds, love with abandon and pursue despite the obstacles.

A few types I find particularly helpful and what mine looked like:

THE UNCONDITIONAL SUPPORTER: The person who supports you no matter what. You know you can count on them to go with you wherever you go and with whatever idea you have. Even when they express doubt, it is in the most supportive way they can create. They are loyal to a fault and will always be by your side.

I have found this person to be the one I look to when the days are getting long. When the days feel like a never-ending stream of tasks and doing and being and I wonder if it's worth it. This person tells me it is - what I am doing is for the best and I need to keep doing it.

THE CHEERLEADER: unfailing, annoying at times, always positive and upside finding.... your cheerleader. Your cheerleader will root for you when you are down, encouraging the rebound. They will scream in ecstasy when you are up and laud your accomplishments without reservation. They recommend you to everyone they know, they talk you up when you demure and they make literal and figurative banners for you.

The cheerleader will remind you, you are promotion worthy. This continuous rah-rah of your awesomeness will keep you smiling and reminding you people are in the crowd and on your side. In my life, this person is a constant source of "you are so awesome, I love how you get to do what you do and help people" usually followed by "I told my friend so and so about you and they are excited to get in touch about xyz you are doing or know about." I love it. I love how she is out there telling people about me even when I am not.

THE ANALYST AKA THE FACTS DUDE: Every idea I have is answered with, "yeah but is it viable? Will it make money/get increased audience/make sense in your schedule/take away from what you love most...and what do you know about it, let me look up some information and see if it's worth it." This is the person who goes bonkers when I simply buy the new car instead of spending 3 months researching all the information about all the available cars in the range I am looking and developing the best option.

Frankly working like that makes me nauseous, but I love knowing people who love to do this kind of analysis. I once bought a car based on the commercial. I loved the commercial. It was for the Pontiac G6 when it first came out. They had a strong confident woman in kick ass heels in a dark grey model with the fully retractable sun roof.... I decided to be her. Within a week I had gone to Pontiac dealership and came home with the exact model right down to the color. Then I bought the heels.

The analyst in my life at the time, my second husband was none too pleased with my action. But I was in impetuous love. And it worked, until I decided I wanted a Jeep. This time I alerted him and he did all the research and we compromised. I got what I wanted, he got what he wanted.

THE RISK ASSESSOR: the dude (dude is asexual in case you haven't noted yet. I am from California, despite my current Midwest zip code, everyone is dude. Always have been, always will be dude), who tells you everything that is or possibly could be wrong with your idea, venture or decision.

You want to use this one sparingly.

If you have a lot of these people in your strike team, you will never, never, never get your rebellion ignited. They will keep dousing it with water telling you that you'll get burned, the fire will spread and burn the town down or tell you the wood is too wet or the wrong kind.

The best use is to find the weak points in your plan, idea or vision. This person is amazing at this. And tell them this is what you are looking for. It isn't an insult. Some people are super good at this – there is an entire field of work out there focused on optimization, risk assessment and the like. This is a fabulous skill to be able to access.

I have more than one person I will use in this, at different stages of where I am with an idea. The first level is the harshest. I'll run an idea by her and see what she thinks then take notes as she rips it to shreds. She will find every possible down side, question I do not yet have an answer to and opportunity I have missed and tell me all about it. It is never a direct personal attack – it is out in the open and I want to identify them.

At that point, I can move forward. I have actions to take.

Once I have closed all the gaps I can see, I go to person 2. Person 2 tends to be just as harsh, but from a different direction aka fresh perspective. From here you can see where your loose ends, frayed facts and missing info is. I rely on this person for the fine detail. They see the minutiae, the nuance and the relationships I would have missed without seeing it fail the first time.

The balance between these two in my life has proven invaluable. They don't even know each other. But I do and I love that they will support me this way.

This can be a single person, you don't need more than 1. As I said, use sparingly. Look for a refined combination of detail and sledgehammer perspective. They're both worthy reviews.

THE CREATIVE AKA YOUR MUSE: Who do you dream with? Probably your muse. Consider who this person is in your world. I have a few. My son is a great one. He is currently 10 and a big thinker. He has lots of stories, ideas and questions about the world. His viewfinder is expanding and for him it means challenging what has become "normal". At ten he has his own rebellion happening and it's about justice on a world scale, not just being pissy with mom or dad. I kinda dig it.

So yes, he sees things and it inspires me. For example, the other day we were driving by a large corporate location in our town. He was quiet as he looked at it but I could see wheels turning. He then says, "mom I don't get why people would go there and sit in little boxes and work all day. Seriously, why would they do that, there are so many better ways to get things done!"

Yeah, my heart swelled with a bit of pride as I mentally back patted and gave myself an attamom.

I informed him I used to occupy a box within that very building when he was born and until he had turned 5. "I am so glad you got out, how can we help other people see how horrible that is?" My favorite part of that statement was the ownership he was choosing to take. But it also served as what I call a "muse moment".

Muse moments are when the creative or muse member of your strike team helps something snap into awareness, being or clarity – or all three at once.

This muse moment was I had muddled up my mission. I had spread myself too thin and though I was chasing my dream still, I was trying to chase it in 4 different directions. Here is what I mean:

In 2012, I went in to business for myself as a life coach with the idea that people don't have to settle for the accepted path in life – there was a way to find true optimal happiness in daily life by being authentically you, not some commercial version of what you were supposed to be.

Then along the way: I started getting people wanting how to be a life coach help, healing, numerology reports, marketing support and free stuff. I tried to be all for everyone. I felt like nothing for no one.

My son's question pulled me right back on track – that muse moment crystallized what had been troubling me for a while: I was doing too much and it wasn't what I really wanted to be doing. From there I could refocus, get some coaching and re-center on my purpose – leading in part to writing this book.

THE TECH GENIUS: the dude who knows or is interested in finding the best way to tech up your idea. The old "there's an app for that" dude. Or even better, "I can create a custom, proprietary, unique just for you app for that" dude.

Your tech genius can be as straightforward as your web designer, but I have found real genius in my information systems manager. He looks at all the functions I need and works to integrate them in the best way possible. I am right this every moment amid a website update and looking at the best integrations from my website to accomplish the highest-level service I want to provide.

Or rather, my tech genius is looking at this. He's awesome. I can explain what I want to have happen. He then tells me how it can happen. I usually then ask how much it will cost. Then we develop the right plan to meet needs AND budget.

In a way, the tech genius on your strike team also serves as a muse. But a very specific kind of the muse, focused on your technology.

YOU: the most important part of your strike team. You can't lose you. You must, and I rarely say must in this way, you MUST maintain who you are and why you are doing what you are doing always. Your vision is the ignition for this rebellion and it is your life that you are rebelling for. It is your life you are creating, the lifestyle you crave. Your rebellion can't become some twisted reproduction of someone else's. You must fight off any attempted coups and stay strong in the ignition process. It can be easy to fall prey to doubt, but you are your best strike team member to diffuse that bomb. This is your purpose and you need to stay on it.

Igniting on Purpose

I grew up in the mountains in California and if you pay any attention at all you will know large forests in California routinely go up in flame. Wildfires are no joke. Both of my brothers have served on wildland fire fighter (WFF) crews and my older younger brother (think about it for a sec) still serves and is working his way up the ranks making us proud, right now he is training crews to be as badass as he was trained to be.

Essentially there are three kinds of fires: controlled burn, natural causes (lightning), and "some dumbass did something so fucking stupid we wonder how they got dressed this morning". Arsonists fall into category 3.

The kind of purposeful ignition I am referring to with your purpose and enacting this rebellion in your world is a hybrid between a controlled burn and natural causes. This happens sometimes in the forest: lightning will strike and the forest goes up, but the WFF teams let it go because it is good for the forest and there are no hazards being created. In this scenario, these are monitored and managed by people who know their shit: there are strike teams ready to go if needed.

When your idea or vision strikes, it is a bit like a lightning strike encouraged to burn on the path you want it to burn on. You let it go on purpose and you feel more purposeful. Think about the last time you felt truly in control: you decided, acted and enjoyed the results. How did that feel?

Pretty fucking good, right?

You felt in charge, on purpose, on fire even and ignited.

When you ignite your rebellion, this is the feeling you are going for, and it'll be a big deal. A big fucking deal.

Igniting this fire starts with that first action you take. It is fanned by the right people on your strike team. They are all gathered around your flame encouraging it to roar. They are all, in their own ways, excited about this new path you are taking and though they may not get it completely at times, you are happy and strong and that's what matters most.

The most important person in your ignition process is you: you are the accelerant, fuel and spark. Without you valuing your idea or vision at the highest levels, action on that energy and recruiting only the best to support you, you won't see the rebellion through to the end.

You deserve better.

Five things that will serve to deliver that spark to the rebellion:

1. A powerful passion fueled idea (see chapter 1)

2. Getting rid of ideas and beliefs that hold you back (see beginning of chapter 2)

3. Taking the first action from your vision

4. Building a powerful strike team to support your ignition while Valuing you and your vision

5. Loving the hell out of the people around you because you love you that much.

Chapter 3:

Leading the Rebellion - Your Manifesto

A vision is fabulous, but it is just clouds in the sky without some detail behind it. And there aren't many people who can offer the level of detail you need. In fact, there is only one: you.

You must be done letting others paint the pictures of your life – you must take charge and lead your rebellion.

There are a few actions which immediately support this:

1. Getting rid of magazine subscriptions

2. Cutting out Self Help Talk Shows

3. Taking a Social Media Hiatus

4. Letting a lifelong friend who is always a cruel critic go

5. Stop comparing your insides to other people's outsides

How do these actions help? Let's look at them in order:

Let go of Magazine Subscriptions:

Magazines are awesome. You don't have to be done with them forever, but they are the paper version of unrealistic expectations. They showcase perfect homes, recipes requiring a chef's kitchen, relationship advice working only if you are paired with your cat, bodies photoshopped and edited to cartoon like proportions, and all kinds of products you MUST have to be simply okay.

Put them on hold, give them to a shelter, donate them somewhere they'll be entertainment at least for a short period and figure out which you miss.

At one point, I was receiving almost 20 magazines a month. I didn't have enough time to read all of them let alone do anything they were suggesting. I had a variety of genres: news, fashion, health, entertainment, cooking, travel, parenting and sports. They stacked up on my coffee table and every time I looked at them I felt a little drained – even by simply not reading them I felt like I wasn't keeping up.

I let them go and currently have 0 magazine subscriptions. Z-E-R-O. I don't miss any of them. When I need something specific, I look for it. I periodically get a magazine from the rack at the store. I don't feel behind. I don't feel disconnected. I love paging through them and do, but I don't feel the compulsion to have them always streaming in and going unread in an attempt to live someone else's life – I get to make conscious decisions about what I want.

Cutting out Self Help Talk Shows:

They are fun: listening to other people tell you what's hot in fashion, how to make the best romance ever or comparing your tragic storyline to theirs and feeling superior. Self Help Talk shows birth reality TV. We get some glorious vicarious sense of wellbeing by listening to someone else be all fucked up and being able to position our life as better.

Maybe it is. But instead of worrying about whether your life is better or worse than someone else's – cutting these shows out for a bit means you must ask yourself what is going well or not going well as compared to the lifestyle you truly want. In other words, how are you thriving?

You are left to analyze your life against the life you want, not the life someone else is living.

Taking a Social Media Hiatus:

We don't see the reality of daily living on social media. We see what others choose to share. Sometimes those shares are full of gloom and doom and we can feel superior. Other times they are optimistic, happy, maybe even a mite braggy and we feel shitty, like we don't measure up. Neither case is you. You are not better or worse than – you are living your life.

Social media is great if you can take it with a grain of salt. I compare it to sitting and watching a crowd of people – love me some people watching – and making decisions about the kind of person that person is based on a singular moment. First, why am I judging? Second, who cares?

Unless the person is harming someone else in some shape or form, how they live is none of my business – noooooooooone. Say it with me, "How they live their life is none of my business. I have things in my life more deserving of my attention."

There it is. We sometimes use other people's lives as distractions to living our own. Social media is this nice little technology window allowing us to peak in on others' lives. We can use it to distract us from the reality happening in the moment, like right now. And now, and now.... you get it.

Taking a social media hiatus is a good way to gauge how much you are allowing social media to influence your perspective. Take one day: sun up to sun down.

During the space created: focus on you and what you are doing and needing and ignoring. Go about your day as you normally would only without social media to check while you wait, to browse while you toilet or distract you from a list of things you want to get done. You will begin to see what is important and what details you want in your vision over what you don't.

Observe how you feel different.

Letting a lifelong friend who always plays the cruel critic go:

Sometimes you just have to say F off. Ask yourself why you are hanging on to one friend who is always critical – maybe not of you directly, but of life in general. Sometimes known as Downer Debby or Negative Neil, this person is an energy drain every single time you are around them.

It blows big time to see their number pop up in your caller ID, you force yourself not to hide if you see them in the store, you invite them to things only out of obligation – not in true desire to hang with them. In other words, this friendship has turned into a habit you need to break in a big way.

Being a leader in your rebellion means you need to be rigorously honest about the kinds of energies you allow in your world. If you have someone consistently bringing out in you the kind of energy described, it's time to shift your approach. It's time to be honest with yourself about what is the highest good.

Once you decide to let that person go, you may have to do nothing more. Making that decision gives you the resolve to say no to spending time with them. I had an acquaintance attempting to become a friend a few years ago. At first, I thought it was great: shared interests, funny convos and similar views on the world. As time went on I realized all conversations were centered on her issues, her frustrations and there was always a request for advice or help in the middle. And she was way more willing to whine than act to fix anything.

I made the decision not to pursue the friendship. Then, our schedules didn't seem to mesh up, I kept missing calls and so did she. She went on a trip and when she came back there was busyness. I found it highly interesting to observe – I didn't avoid her and didn't confront it. Today we are acquaintances who can say hi and have a conversation, but there isn't any intimacy to it. I'm fine with it – and she seems to be too.

Our energies were not naturally aligned and they fell naturally when we weren't forcing it.

If you don't find it as serendipitous as I, you may have to confront the situation – or be forced to by the other person. Think about what you'd want to hear, think about how they hear things and deliver your position accordingly. Will it hurt them? Maybe. But you are leading your life and making decisions in your highest and best good about who you want in your world.

Taking negative dialogue out of your life removes both a distraction and a perspective not truly you. It also allows you to see with more accuracy what you really want, think or feel about things happening to you and others. This clarity you are left with adds more detail to the kick ass lifestyle vision you began with. It just gets better from here.

Stop comparing your insides to other people's outsides

Here to tell you: what is going on inside and outside a person don't always match. Think of the times you have put on a smile when you didn't want to or when you pretended to be sorry when you weren't. What is happening inside us is not what we show the world in every moment.

A couple of colleagues and I were talking about honesty as we sat down to our meeting for the day. It was an offhand remark like, "if I'd only been able to say what I was really thinking" that got us asking why we couldn't. So, we tried it. For the next hour, the three of us responded with what was really on our minds and not the filtered version. Things like "dumbest idea I have ever heard" were shared and we got a lot done. It really was a great meeting.

In daily living, we can aspire to this level of transparency, but we won't always receive or achieve it. Our humanity and sense of self-preservation will block it. There would have to be a humongous paradigm shift across the global landscape for this to happen.

Instead, take control of what we can do: shift our own paradigms. Before we see someone else's life and compare it to how we feel we need to remember the measuring stick isn't working.

In fact, we are better served in spending energy on comparing our current existence to our vision of the kickass life we want to be living and seeing how we are doing. It is a more accurate measurement of our sense of happiness and satisfaction, how we are thriving. Way better than checking out someone else's outside and comparing to the bloody mess of fears and insecurities which shift into overdrive as soon as we open the door to our insides.

Without a super weird filtered view and with the enhanced clarity on your vision you can see even more and see more action you can take to build your best life in the time you are living. Maybe none of these things apply to you – ask yourself what is influencing your filter. Where are you always looking for validation? That is the habit you need to drop now.

What you Value Most

All this de-filtering and vision enhancing activity allows you to see what you Value Most.

One night I was prepping for a call with my coach and I was feeling straight up overwhelmed. I started writing down all the areas I was spending time in. I had a long list including everything from business travel to grocery shopping. Next, I grouped similar things together: my son, extended family, personal health, community, work and spiritual work. Then I wrote each item in each group from highest priority to lowest priority by group.

From there I immediately saw a huge imbalance. I was spending a ton of time in community giving and work. I was spending way less time with my son by comparison. If I were to rank the groups in order: most to least valued, I'd have put my spiritual health at the top with work at the bottom.

I examined it again for draining items and then for what was missing. I quickly came to see there was a line I could draw straight across my entire list and what was below the line needed to go.

I reviewed all of this with my coach and developed an action plan for the tougher items on my must go list. I had to release things like volunteering with the Boys and Girls Club, doing less service work for my recovery organization and business travel. Over the course of the next few months I got lighter and lighter as those items faded.

In revisiting my lists over and over I realized I had created a picture of what I valued most in life. I clarified what I meant by each:

Spiritual Health: I possess a daily practical and spiritual routine connecting me to source energy and am conscious of the influences I allow into my life. I am solely responsible for my actions and act accordingly. I am physically, emotionally and spiritually active. I have freedom and adventure in my world constantly. I love me.

My Son: I spend regular, present time with my son doing things we both enjoy. I encourage his passions and work to inspire discipline where he needs it most. We adventure together. I tell him I love him.

My Extended Family: I support my family where needed and within my means. I am available for them and interested in what is happening with them. I take responsibility where my strength is a help and let go when it isn't. I am present at activities and celebrations whenever possible. We accept each other for who we are. I tell them I love them.

My Career: I stay clear on my mission. I focus on serving my clients in the highest vibration possible. I am consistent, dependable and direct. I am fiscally responsible and act with the highest integrity in all dealings. I source responsibly and act consciously with all product and tools I use. I demonstrate freedom and independence and inspire rebellion. I love how I work.

Here are the steps to take to get to this level of detail for you (Pro Tip: use a spreadsheet program to construct this to make it easy to move things around):

1. Identify everything occupying your time now.

2. Group the items by commonality.

3. Rank the items within each group from highest to lowest in importance to you.

4. Rank the groups you have formed from highest to lowest priority.

5. Identify what you are not doing and needs to be added to each group.

6. Re-order with the wish list items added.

7. Look at what you want to be free of by group.

8. Work to get free of the things you want to be free of.

9. Add in the things you want to be doing.

10. Continue adjusting.

11. As you revisit your list, further define each group into a mission style statement for those values or priorities in your life.

12. Frame your mission statements and put them where you will see them every single day.

Having done this, you have created a super clear system for yes or no in your life. As opportunities or situations show up in your world you can ask yourself where they fit, or how your values are impacted by the decision to say yes or no.

A client once struggled with whether to take a particular job. She had been wanting to focus on the business she was starting but her personal life was forcing a move and she needed additional steady income.

She had two great offers to consider. Each offered very different potential and very different working environments. She saw beauty in both and was undecided about which appealed most. Not a bad situation to be in.

She requested my support in her decision making and I asked her how each stacked up against her values. We had already gone through the Aligning Priorities exercise and woven through the details of them. She wasn't yet in the habit of decision making with them yet.

We looked at her opportunities against the backdrop of her values and it became clearer. She wanted to take some more time with them and did some homework on it. Later that night I got a text sharing her decision. The decision crystallized the more she looked at her values and the respective opportunities.

We can waste a lot of time in indecisiveness without a clear vision of where we are going and what is most important to us along the way. We don't need to do that. Getting clear on what is most important to us is a vital component to stepping onto the dangerous path of living the way we want to.

"Where You Focus Will Flourish"

I love this expression. It's true. Where I spend time, money and energy, flourishes. Where I don't, dies.

When I know my values, and have a clear vision for what I want and actions I am willing to take to get it, I can focus on the things I really want to focus on: what matters most and contributes to building the kind of lifestyle I want to live. I ask myself "does this get me closer or further away from the life I want to love?" and get a super clear answer.

As a kid, I was never asked what I valued most or what kind of lifestyle I wanted to live. There was discussion around jobs I wanted, kind of man I'd marry or where I wanted to live and what my house would look like. There wasn't a focus on how I'd flourish in my life in all those scenarios. It just wasn't how we talked about it then.

As I grew older, it became like hiking up a mountain and finding an expansive vista at the top entirely shifting your perspective on your place in the world.

I know many people who still haven't taken that hike. Their focus remains on the right job, the right person, the right house...and on and on. The focus is less on "how to create a life I love" and more on "how I can get things I love".

Where you focus will flourish, knowing where you want to focus and being conscious about it matters.

The Mantle of Leadership

As the weight of the mantle of leadership settles on to your shoulders an empowering light spreads across your being. The light can brighten your path, it won't blind you. It will illuminate the steps you need to take for your vision to become a plan to convert into action.

This mantle will feel heavy, but not burdensome. More comfortable than confining. It will feel like the blanket of love and support you require for yourself to feel on purpose. The mantle of leadership is an internally facing entity concerned with you and you alone.

You are charged with leading you now. The most important leadership assignment you could accept.

You will rebel against it. You will fight for the way things used to be. Your ego will tell you, you are being dumb, everything is fine or was fine the way it was. You'll find fierce enemies in doubt, worry, fear, anger and guilt as you lead your warrior tribe of one down the dangerous path of living the life most authentic to you.

You will aid yourself through these battles to win the war against settling. You'll shed the mantle of expectation, you'll assume the mantle of leading yourself and you will find yourself creating a path consisting the most kickass of elements. You will learn a lot of about your own stamina and strength and you will be amazed.

How to Lead your Personal Rebellion:

1. Add Detail to Your Vision

2. Live by what you Value Most

3. Remember where you Focus Will Flourish

4. Get Comfortable with the Weight of the Mantle of Leadership

5. Love your Leader as you Love yourself: Infinitely

Chapter 4:

Survival Skills and Super Strengths

Hey, you are pretty stinkin' amazing.

What is your immediate gut level reaction this statement?

Do you demure, resist or deflect?

Perhaps you immediately respond with a counter compliment.

If you are completely comfortable with it, good.

Because it is true. I don't mean in the superficial context. I mean in the think deeply blow your frickin mind kind of way.

However, many years ago, roughly 9 months before you were born, you were just a concept. Then biology happened and you became a group of cells and from there your being came into existence. On a spiritual level, your energy was connected to the fabric before your conception, waving around out there, processing it's previous incarnation experience and selecting its next target life. How you were born to the parents you were born to, the country, the socioeconomic and all the things shaped you and influenced your life, are amazing.

So yeah, anyway you look at it, you are amazing.

Many of us need a little more: we need details and information and specifics telling us why we, ourselves are uniquely amazing rather than the generic "you are a spiritual being having a physical experience" kind of way.

What this is not: an ego stroking. I don't have time for ego stroking and you have better ways to spend your time and energy. I am not a big fan of the everybody wins philosophy. I am a big fan of everyone having some stuff in their arsenal they kick ass with.

If you are looking for an ego stroking, I just think you are looking at this all wrong. A big ego isn't sustainable. It requires more and more over time to keep it fed and dumb and happy. Heavy emphasis on the dumb.

Instead, how about an honest assessment of what is righteously cool about you. This is about things you are good at, talents you possess and the things you do making you feel like the muthafucking king of the goddamned world.

As a child, I loved to write. Absolutely loved words and prose. I spent hours in books and enjoyed the power of creating my own works. At some point, I Lost it. Capital L lost it. It went away and I quit looking at it as a strength.

I had a friend who was quite gifted with the pen and quill. Her genre was fantasy and she could write incredibly detailed, rich stories full of adventure and intrigue. I compared myself to her and found myself lacking. I couldn't write like her (never mind that I didn't want to), so clearly it wasn't a strength. I didn't tell anyone this. I didn't ask for validation or dissuasion. I just decided it and I quit trying to write.

Today I love to write and am consistently praised for my ability to turn a phrase in the written word. Am I the best?

Yes.

Hahaha

No, I am not, but I am confident in my abilities. This is a strength for me and I claim it.

A few others are: humor, grit, speaking, teaching, risk taking, motherhood, merchandising, loving people completely, cutting loses when they need to be cut, diligence and giving.

What have you been praised for?

Make a list – these are strengths as others perceive them.

Now throw it away. Who cares? Doesn't matter.

What do YOU perceive as strengths?

I did an exercise once where I wrote down all the things I loved about me. It was SUPER hard at first. I thought it was dumb. I am not a fan of standing in front of the mirror and telling me I love me. I certainly didn't want to look at myself in the mirror and tell me all the great things about me. I perceived it as weak ass new age bullshit serving as imitation masturbation for our egos.

Yes, I felt strongly against it.

I was in a group coaching environment and I went along with the nonsense. And guess what.... I bet you can guess the end of this story.

Yep. It worked. It fucking worked.

I found my energy spiking as I read the list to the group. Uncomfortable at times, not from a BS perspective but from a "omg this is the first time I am claiming this" kind of place, I felt amazing.

I added a shed load of strengths to my list to include my favorite: I am SASSY. There is no small amount of sass within me and it brings me all kinds of fun experiences. It gets me into trouble and it gets me into fun. It lets me play with my kid and fight for what I need in a way that works for me. I love my sass.

Look within.

Your strengths are there waiting to be recognized, given a name. Names have power, speaking them have power, seeing their presence within you has some MOFOing POWER. This power is inside right now to be claimed. Claim them now.

Conventional wisdom might be telling you to be humble. To let others find them. Common sense says your strengths don't need to be paraded about like a show dog. Strengths are there to be of use when needed and otherwise ignored and even diminished when praised. Let's use uncommon sense instead.

My son was singing on the couch. He has a gorgeous voice. Not just mother's bias, he really does. My partner complimented him, "whoa dude, you have a great voice." My son replied immediately, "no I don't". And like super matter of factly too! As if he could just deny it and it would be true.

I didn't teach him to deny his strengths. In fact, I have been asking him to embrace it and sing in a show or a musical. He refused to sign up for a solo in his musical last year. I don't push, he needs to be comfortable and I am also teaching him no means no with this.... but OMG. He has a beautiful voice and I wish he'd share his strength instead of denying it.

We demure in a weak ass attempt at survival, not recognizing survival is about using strengths, not resisting them.

Let me repeat, survival is about using your strengths. And Thriving is honoring them.

The University of Pennsylvania's Positive Psychology Department has, in short, been studying what is right with people. In other words, the ideas about how people thrive instead of focusing on what is wrong with them and fixing it. I love this.

They have a strengths assessment tool anyone can take for free which assesses 24 Character Strengths. The father of positive psychology, Martin Seligman writes about his assessment and the work that led up to it in his book "Authentic Happiness: Using the New Positive Psychology to Realize Your Potential for Lasting Fulfillment". Find the tool at www.authentichappiness.org VIA Survey of Character Strengths.

This survey and its results aren't a typing, they are a ranking of 24 strengths we all possess. It ranks them from most present to least present. This supports my personal theory that can't is kinda BS. I don't mean "I can't lift 450 pounds" on day 1 of your weight lifting program. I am talking about the excuses like, "I can't be patient, I don't possess that strength" or "I just can't be on time, not in my wiring".

I don't buy it. I believe you possess the capability, it may just be a little weaker in you and you, being aware of your shortcoming can perhaps use other strengths to compensate. But it starts with awareness, right?

The Value of the External View

There is some value in asking others where you are strong. The outside perspective can support your quest to break through the expectations of others. Seems twisted at first, but go with me for a minute. Because it matters HOW you do this.

We have internalized a lot of story lines along the way from our birth to now. Don Miguel Ruiz refers to this as programming in his book "The Four Agreements". From the moment of our birth we are handed the "how to's" of life according to our surroundings. Our parents, family and environment as we grew up, our school system, our friends, teachers, coaches, mentors and anyone we encountered along the way planted a version of how we are supposed to act in our being.

Doesn't mean it was right. Does not mean we are thriving under those conditions.

I grew up without much and believed myself to be unworthy. I did everything to fit in I could but always felt like the kid who didn't get her locker combination on the day everyone else did. There were experiences and interactions with people along the way substantiating this thought. I turned to alcohol in my early teens for help and it "worked" until I was about 28 when I realized it had made me dependent on it. My alcoholism was a mask for the continued belief in my unworthiness – alcohol gave me false strength.

The outside perspective helped to me to see what they saw: potential. It came in all forms:

- Performance reviews at work

- Friends with compliments

- Colleagues asking to be mentored

- And answers to my direct question of "what do you think my strengths are?"

I didn't have to take every response as the absolute truth. I was aware enough not to, but I did receive insight I could process and validate from within. The external perspective serves to enhance the internal when used correctly.

This is why coaching is such an invaluable resource: a coach doesn't tell you what to do. A coach helps you discover the truths and strengths within through perspective and accountability as you pursue clear goals and objectives.

If you surround yourself with expectations of conformity, your internal energy will feel like you've placed it in a vessel one or more sizes too small. Imagine going to the costume shop knowing you are a Size 10. You know this to be true about you and there is not argument or question. All your clothing in your closet is a size 10, even your shoes are a size 10. This is true for you in the most absolute way possible.

You get to the shop and the owner tells you, you are an 8. In that particular shop, you are an 8 and that is all there is to it. He can tell by looking at the makeup of your body and height and weight you are not a 10, but an 8. Not only are you an 8, but everyone else is an 8 as well so if you try to be a 10, well...you will be different and different is scary and not good and you just don't want to do that. You put up an initial fight, but he wears you down and you squeeze into the 8.

It sucks.

It is too small, it pinches and squeezes in the wrong areas. You can't walk right, forget about reaching for anything. The zipper is in the back and you can't reach it to get the thing off, though you know it is there. Eventually, this constricted feeling becomes normal and you adapt. You get smaller so it feels better. You slouch or loose unhealthy weight and it begins to feel like it fits. The arms are still too short and the legs ride up and lord knows it is crawling into places nothing should crawl, but you accept this as your jam now.

Bullshit.

You let that dude convince you your truth was wrong. We do this, we let others tell us what is true despite our truth within screaming at us to do different. Our scream becomes a whisper over time as we let the voices of others drown it out. We hear it on the wind and strain to figure out what the odd sound is. We feel a niggling tingle in the back of our mind like we forgot something and then carry on. We know there is something.... but what is it?

We look at our size 8 life and vaguely remember a time when we felt like more. More is now missing. We crave it, but then deny ourselves, pushing it down because it doesn't fit everyone's idea of right. "The costume feels okay now, keep wearing it.", you tell yourself.

This is where the right outside perspective is pure genius. The right outside perspective can help you see the constrictions you have allowed. It can reveal what has been hidden within and let it out. It can help you with the zipper you saw so long ago and forgot existed. It can show you the strengths of being who you want to be, who you know you can be, stepping back out of the reduction into your full being. It can unzip your zipper and allow you to shed the costume.

And there are those glorious strengths.

That is the difference between conforming to outside perspective and allowing perspective to support you. Which one are you surrounding yourself with?

Finding Your Zipper

When I recovered from alcoholism, I spent a lot of time surrounding myself with people who wanted to support my stepping into the right sized costume. Outside of the recovery system, I found myself attracted to people who promoted authenticity over conformity. This is when I started looking for the zipper in my costume.

I found less tolerance for people who wanted me to pursue some idea of success, happiness and myself which began with concepts like "they" or "should" or "have to". Instead I looked for the outliers.

I looked for the ideas and people I felt truly connected with. I took a bunch of classes to gain information and quickly remembered I could take from those what I wanted and leave the rest. Someone teaching a class doesn't mean they are the final authority...especially a personal development class. Take what you want and leave the rest – use what works for you and let go of everything else.

I began to focus on using my strengths every day. I found myself feeling happier, more excited to do things I had always been doing. The job I held didn't feel like such a burden, while at the same time feeling less and less connected to who I really was. When it came time to leave it, it felt natural. It felt like the right sized step to take.

People around me helped me find my zipper and the actions I took unzipped it. It didn't happen in a weekend workshop or a 3-hour class. It happened with consistent effort and a committed desire to live the life I really wanted to be living. The 3-hour classes helped, and the workshops had their place, but they were not the beginning and end of the answer. The real work happened in coaching, in consistent daily action and putting my strengths to work every day.

Daily Do Gooding

You are in charge. You have your strengths now use them. You can honor the discoveries you have made or you can dismiss them. If you don't believe you don't have to conform yet, keep reading.

There are times you must start even when you aren't convinced it is true. The action can help you prove or disprove the idea. Seriously, sometimes what you try just isn't the right approach. It doesn't mean your idea is wrong, it means you must use your grit and try again – or try until it's time to try differently. Angela Duckworth talks about this idea of grit in her aptly named book Grit: The Power of Passion and Perseverance, released in 2016.

Using your strengths daily actually increases happiness. Especially when it comes to your vocation. People who use their strengths daily report overall higher levels of wellbeing than those that do not[1]. That seems like common sense, right?

Yet, we all know someone who isn't– maybe even us. Even though it seems silly. Why wouldn't we use our strengths every day?

One reason is we are told not to. From their earliest days, social kids are told they must behave and follow all the rules exactly as written to be perceived as good in the classroom. Sit quietly, raise your hand, don't wiggle. For a truly social kid interested in what everyone else is doing and keen to observe and interact with the world around them, this feels like a prison sentence.

My son was this kid and I am very grateful to his second-grade teacher for noticing and working with him. My son would

[1] Adapted from Gallup comprehensive study of wellbeing of more than 150 countries covering 98% of the world's population.

burst with energy as he watched the world around him unfolding. She encouraged the kids to get up and wiggle when they needed to, my son went a step further.

When he'd feel energy welling up inside, he'd stand up next to his desk and run in place. We learned he is a kinetic learner – one who learns better when moving. If he could run in place while she was sharing information or drilling on math facts or spelling words, he'd be able to spit out the answers. If forced to sit still, not so much.

I see this in the courses I teach as well. One is a course I teach training Customer Service Professionals. Yes, those guys and gals on the other end of the phone you get irritated with because their company isn't doing what you want, or you have a pleasant conversation with when you get married or have an address change. In this course, we have a blend of credit students who are pursuing a tech support degree and continuing education students. All are eligible to receive a certificate at the end of the 13-week course which runs daily for 4.5 hours.

It is an intense course, we treat it like a work environment with attendance, dress code and participation requirements. There are deadlines and projects and team building. Some love it and some get through it. As in a workplace, we work to accommodate optimal working environment. If someone needs something to work more effectively, we try to make it happen: one is motion. I encourage students to stand up when they practice calls, get up and walk or move during instruction times or doodle if they need the fine motor motion. The students recognizing this in themselves and acting on it are more engaged. They are using their strengths.

Every day, consider how your strength can come into the game as an asset. The game being your life and your goal to win it according to your unique path.

Recently a client discovered her top strength to be playfulness and joy. She was having a rough period in her life having relocated to a new country, new job and promptly encountering all manner of not only culture shock but outright thievery. She was despairing as to how to handle it and we decided to try consciously using her top strength – focusing only on it to improve her days.

The suggestion immediately resonated as she shared she had already been complimented for her lightness, humor and how easy she was to talk to in the workplace. She went from asking me how to be happier to creating her own exercises to increase her happiness in a matter of days. Instead of conforming to the doom and gloom environment and culture she was surrounded with, she embraced her difference and stepped into her true energy of lightness and fun.

She recently expressed concern over staying in the location for longer than her initial commitment period. She didn't want the oppressive nature of her surroundings to convert her into "one of them". A harsh, slow working, critical and unhelpful person. While it may possible, the better question is whether it is probable?

I don't think so. Playfulness and levity is her top strength. I think she will always shine if she honors it daily for herself. There is an adage, "wherever you go, there you are". It is meant as a warning in the circles I have heard it spoken, but isn't it also a message of hope?

The most important thing you carry with you daily are your strengths. The more you use them, the more they grow and flourish and come to the headline section of your life through your actions. There is so much focus on fixing what is wrong with us. Where I live I can't sneeze without getting some sort of herbal remedy, healing energy or yoga pant clad wannabe guru telling me what kind of cleanse I need.

Ironically, I believe in all those remedies. I use herbs, I eat organic, I do yoga, I use healing energy – heck I am the co-founder of the Midwest Reiki Festival – but I don't want to do all this your way. I'm good with doing it mine. My top strength is industriousness followed by spirituality. I think that means I should be a monk? Obviously. But I checked and they have too many rules.

Plus, they don't seem to want single parents in there.

Anyway, those top strengths combine with the totality of who I am and what I bring to the table every day.

You need to know what yours are and bring them to your table every day. This is how authentic, awesome, living by your rules not someone else's rules rebels get to thrive.

Here are 5 ways to identify your strengths and bring them full on every day:

1. Visit authentichappiness.org and take the VIA Survey of Character Strengths. While you are there, also check out the Grit assessment. Both will provide you some real insight into what you are working with. It's free, you do have to create a log in – takes less than 30 seconds.

2. Pick your toughest, most onerous segment of your day to rework around your strength. How can your crappy part get kickass by leveraging your strength?

3. Look at the work you do and figure out how your strength is applied. If it absolutely is not, get out as quickly as you can and find a position where you can. Go back to school if you must, take extreme action.

4. Share your strength and your plan to focus on it with your mentor, manager, spouse, partner, best friend, children, parents.... everyone you encounter daily. Now it's out there and you have asked it to be part of who you present to them – they'll help you act on it.

5. Love your strength by telling it thank you. Every night look at the ways your strength played a role in the kind of day you lived. It helped you kick ass, it deserves the praise. Since it is part of you, you are also loving the ever-loving shit out of you in the process.

Chapter 5:

When Your Current Life Fights Back

"You'll be on your way up!

You'll be seeing great sights!

You'll join the high fliers

Who soar to great heights.

You won't lag behind, because you'll have speed.

You'll pass the whole gang and you'll soon take the lead.

Wherever you fly, you'll be the best of the best.

Wherever you go, you will top all the rest.

Except when you don't.

Because sometimes, you won't."

Oh, the Places You'll Go – Dr. Seuss

Such a great book, but this has always been my favorite part. This is how life happens sometimes. Life is rocking, you are on top of the fucking world screaming like a banshee on ecstasy and streaking naked through fire. And then it gets hard. The screaming gets whiny, the ecstasy turns into a super bad acid trip and you are hanging upside down in a skirt with no panties on while your class laughs and points.

Sometimes life gets hard. Sometimes it feels like it is fighting back.

You get to roll up your sleeves and renew your focus. Many people more specialized than I in the theories around our reaction to change have put their minds to the task of mapping our emotional cycle around it.

It is basically an upside-down bell curve. On the incline is the initial ecstasy. On the decline is the despair and questioning...and then we settle in.

That downslope is where you can find yourself sometimes. And it feels icky.

How do you handle it now? A few things I have seen (and done):

- Retreat

- Hole up in isolation

- Get manic with bad for you shit

- Get angry as hell and take it out on everyone else

- Decide to binge on super good for yourself stuff until you collapse in exhaustion

- Repress that shit – pretend it isn't real

- Get sick – create the icky feeling in your body

And those are just a few. I have personally done them all...you? Come on be honest.

Well, you don't have to do any of them.

When resistance happens, because it will, the first best thing to do is recognize it. Recognize it happening and allow the detail to come forth. Recognition can be super tough – to admit while you pursue what you want, you are also not wanting it? You may wonder why you are so screwy or what's wrong with you.

Nothing. Nothing is wrong with you. Acknowledge this first. You are fine.

Now it's time to flush out what the resistance is: find its source and what it is trying to protect.

Because really there is the core of resistance: a protection mechanism. It's your ego protecting what is in existence. It's a natural reflex. It's your job as a conscious being now to tell it change is okay and to allow this transition to occur.

The best way I know how to do this is to write it down. Write down all the details of the resistance. Once it is there in black and white (or blue or pink, I don't care what color pen you use, just use it!), you can analyze it. Analyze it to prepare your response. This process allows you to respond – a higher vibe method of approach than a simple reaction. Reacting tends to be more knee jerk when you are dealing with resistance. A response requires thought followed by thoughtful action.

Once you have defeated your own internal resistance, you get to take on external resistance. The number one question to answer here is "does it matter?" Does the person resisting what you are doing, changing or creating even matter?

If they don't, let them go.

If they do, guess what? Yes, thoughtful response and action.

After heavily investing in a Healing Center in 2012 with my time, effort, literal blood, sweat and tears and money I was INVOLVED. I had my practice hosted there, my construction company had built the offices at a loss and I owned the growing store within. I was also the person on the desk most, working there more than anyone else – including the owner.

I realized this was yet another cage I had placed myself in: I was an entrepreneur and loving most of what I was doing, but I was also still entirely too tethered to expectation. There was an expectation of the things I would do as part of the center and I wasn't okay with it. Having reconciled it within, I needed to make the external moves and resistance from others happened.

I was accused of sabotage, being selfish, taking without giving, being disrespectful, abandoning and more. This after I sold the store to the owner at cost and had been running her business daily for almost a year. It would have been easy to get really angry and resentful and let it tear me up. Instead, I analyzed those decisions and realized how horrible some of the business decisions I made were and how to structure myself and my decisions differently in similar environments going forward.

There were three things forming the key to moving through this:

1. Stay clear on what was right for me.

2. Communicate as clearly as I could.

3. Meet in the middle where it was mutually beneficial.

I found those three actions to be paramount to any other when dealing with dissention in the ranks.

It wasn't a fun situation for me: it felt like a daily battle. But it passed. There was a short resurgence when I decided to relocate my business 12 months later but by then, I was so centered in my own vision and what I wanted to create, my communication was even more clear and I could compromise exactly where it made sense from conversation one.

The basic rule to remember as you take these actions is you can't control anyone else. They will act and react how they choose to react and act. There is nothing you can do about it except remain clear on what is right for you, communicate clearly and compromise where it makes sense.

And the truth is, some people won't matter. It won't matter if some people don't agree. You aren't creating your own path to win a popularity contest. You are creating it because it makes sense for you. Some people will have to leave your life.

It's okay to care when that happens. And it's okay not to care. It's okay to tell people to fuck off and get out. Some people will not only not understand, they will move to block you from progress in any way. When my now ex-husband told me I had to choose to continue in my business with restricted hours that worked for him "or else", I had to choose "or else". He wasn't interested in my creating my dream, he was interested in preserving his lifestyle.

My dream was more important to me than his lifestyle. I was clear on what I wanted to create. It was different than what he wanted.

I could communicate it clearly all day long, he didn't want to hear it.

The compromise had been in effect for a while already. I had been trying to work around his schedule and allow him the time and space he wanted for the things he wanted. It wasn't enough.

We ended the relationship.

Making this change to thrive in a world where you have been expected to conform doesn't mean your marriage will end. It doesn't mean you will lose your friends or family. You don't have to lose anyone. It's not a requirement. But it is a possibility. If you are going to lose anyone, I'd guess you can speculate right now on who it will be.

Allow them to surprise you.

Again: Be clear, communicate completely and compromise where you need to. Then let go of what you have to.

Triple D's: Doubt, Discouragement, Depression

Whether it is internal or external resistance occurring, three emotions love to make an appearance when your life decides to fight back against change: Doubt, Discouragement and Depression. These three can be powerful energy sappers and if left to run rampant, can defeat your rebellion. You aren't going to let this happen, right?

Let me hear it, "I'm not going to let the Triple D's defeat my rebellion!" loud and proud my friends, loud and proud.

It would be super cool if simply yelling it was enough.

Instead, you must recognize them when they show up and confront them head on. I have a set of powerful questions I use to defeat these threats to your rebellion:

Doubt:

- What is the worst possible outcome?

- What is the best possible outcome?

- What is the most likely outcome?

Discouragement:

- What have I tried successfully?

- What have I tried unsuccessfully?

- What do I need to let go of?

Depression:

- Do I have the symptoms of clinical depression? (if yes, please seek a therapist trained to treat depression)

- When was the last time I took me time to do something I enjoy just because I enjoy it?

- Have I been consistently doing the 6 happiness habits?

The Six Daily Happiness Habits[2]:

1. Laughing

2. One minute of deep breathing

3. Doing something for someone else

4. Writing three gratitude's daily

5. 20 minutes of physical activity

6. Indulgence – the thing that simply brings joy

Use these questions when you feel one or more of these forms of resistance: it's your life fighting back and you can defeat it. You are in control. You are in charge – we have already talked about it.

---

[2] I learned about these from Valorie Burton, in her Coaching Certification course through the CaPP Institute in 2012 (www.cappinstitute.com). I have been applying and sharing them ever since. Check out Valorie's work, it is fabulous.

In creating your own path, you get to deal with the good and the bad – the momentum and the drag. Not everyone will be happy for you, not everyone will support it. Some will. Some will encourage and promote. And resistance will arrive on all sides.

What you do, how you handle it and how you thrive is 100% in your hands.

Go kick ass like a MOFO.

Chapter 6:

Living Dangerously

Welcome to a new state of being and living. It's awesome. You decided to rock your idea and make it real. You have CHOSEN to thrive in a world that expects you to conform.

Welcome freedom seeking rebel.

You are creating a new normal. This is different than what you have been living. In early days, it will feel fragile. You will regress and progress at a variety of rates and paces. Some days you will wonder if it is worth it. Other days you will wonder why you didn't do it sooner. Eventually, your new normal just becomes normal.

Eventually you will see your former normal as more than slightly surreal. It will feel like a different lifetime. You may even wonder how you did it for so long. This is also normal. It is important to also remember the life you had before was real. It was you and you are capable of it – you are capable of not thriving. Pour your energy not on living in the past and what could and should have happened, but on what is happening and what you are creating next.

The Art of Living Dangerously

About 18 months after I left my corporate job, sold my homes, my husband and I had separated and I was living in a small 1-bedroom apartment in a neighborhood I loved I found myself writing in a coffee shop, just as I had envisioned. I took a sip of a cappuccino and it struck me: I was living my vision. I had achieved what I set out to create.

I reflected on my former life and found it to feel very separate from where I was now. Random memories bounced through my mind:

- Growing up poor and wanting more, always knowing it was possible but not sure how.

- Running the mountains of California, sunbathing on granite boulders in the middle of a lake, swinging on pine trees, bare feet on pine needles.

- Military service and deployments and MRE picnics in Uzbekistan.

- Military working dogs joyfully receiving belly rubs in between shifts.

- The camel spider that chased me in to the MP tent - because they had the big guns and could shoot it.

- Showing the Deputy Commanding General how to use his cell phone so he could call if he got lost on his way back to the states.

- My first marriage and divorce.

- Recovery from alcoholism.

- And on and on.

These moments surfed through my head and I realized those experiences enabled the very moment I was in, sitting there in the café.

As I felt profound delicious gratitude fill me up, it was met with pure unadulterated terror. I had achieved everything in the vision I created with my coach a few years prior. Now what?

The only thing missing was moving to the beach, but honestly that didn't feel like enough. What I needed was a whole new vision.

I realized what I needed was a vision which grew and expanded with my experience instead of a checklist of wants I could tick off as I achieved them.

My big aha was this was about the journey, the experience and the growth in this lifetime – not about the having stuff. It was huge, I felt rocked. I tweeted and blogged and Facebooked my revelation. Then I had to create the new vision. So, I did.

Being Real in a Fake world

One major lesson I learned in this phase of vision realization was not everyone is Real. Not capital R real. Some of them know this and are okay with it – taking pride in their fakeness. Others are simply asleep. They are following the path in front of them and not really questioning anything at all. They buy what everyone else is buying, do what everyone else is doing and copy more than they create.

That's not you. You are here to be Real.

This is the core of your rebellion – being Real – the Real you feel within but haven't fully lived yet.

My realization was, I was getting Real. I was doing what I wanted to do because I wanted to do it, not because it was on the approved or endorsed list. Look around, you will see fake everywhere: synthetic clothing, caked on makeup, steroid muscles, plastic furniture, fake flowers (wtf is this any way!), food that is entirely chemically engineered.... I don't have enough energy to list it all. Just noting those makes me tense.

Choose Real. You may not know what real is for you yet. Keep asking within. You deserve to know. One question I love to ask myself when I encounter an idea about what I "should" do is "who told me this?" It is a Real questioning of where the idea or belief came from and whether it is true for me. Because the next question you ask is, "is it true for me now?"

- Eat Real Food.

- Surround yourself with Real People.

- Purchase Real products.

- Plant Real Flowers and Trees.

Where do you need to get Real right now?

The mythical "there" – you won't find it

I don't believe in a "there". The place where all is perfect and true and right in the world where you get to just stop growing and learning and simply roll around in the fruits of your labor to get "there". It isn't our human experience.

We are here to grow and evolve and experience and try and fail and get up and get dirty and cry and laugh and be messy as hell. We are here to live in a world with poisonous snakes and bright blue waterfalls. What a spectacular fucking place to be.

The idea of a "there" where we just sit back and allow it all to languish is silly. We are here to participate. We can be mindful in our participation: being present, enjoying the moment, allowing things to exist exactly as they are and appreciate them. Not languishing, thriving.

A State of Constant Evolution

Adjust your idea of "there" to be a direction, a vision consistently expanding and adjusting based on what you're learning and experiencing now. Allow it to be a living entity Real for you and allowing you to continue to fully immerse in your human experience. It is expansive always, constrictive never.

A Final Word

The Final Challenge: move beyond surviving, it's time to thrive

I have given you a 5-step flow for thriving in a world that expects you to conform. You have been given insight, actions and mindset adjusting techniques you now apply for them to work. It would be super cool if just reading all of this made it true for you. It's even cooler, it requires active participation from you instead.

Your challenge now is to go do it.

1. Birth your Rebellion: Create your vision for your optimal life. Get clear on what you want, how you want to feel and why you want it.

2. Ignite the Rebellion: Take your first actions. Examine your vision and initiate action from it. Move vision from concept to reality and let the momentum build. Keep fueling your fire and build your team.

3. Lead your Rebellion: Get clear on your priorities, know what is most important to you and share it with your team. Allow them to support you and enhance your vision. Always accept the failures and the fabulous in equal measure – they are yours to grow with.

4. Survival Skills and Super Strengths: Know your areas of strength and where you need help or optimization. Your internal and others' external perspectives won't

always match – it is up to you to decide where it matters and adjust accordingly.

5. When your Current Life Fights Back: Adapt and overcome. Assuming you have flowed powerfully in 1-4, you have all you need to address head on, avoid and quash any resistance. You are equipped. You can deal with internal resistance, external resistance and the threat of Doubt, Discouragement and Depression.

It's time now to Live Dangerously. It's time to thrive in a world that expects you to conform. It's time for the rebellion. The Art of Living Dangerously is about being you, being Real and being on your path. You are equipped to do this with aplomb.

Do be dangerous. Do be rebellious. Do be you.

Welcome Freedom Seeking Rebel. I am glad you are here.

About the Author

Jennifer Murphy is a certified personal and executive coach ruthlessly focused on helping people live awesome lives. She spent a large chunk of her life pursuing other people's ideas of success and while those experiences were sublime in some cases, they weren't the "more" she was seeking and she just never felt full. In 2011, she made the commitment to live life on her terms and everything changed. The life she thrives in today was created.

Her background is 10 years in the US Army as an officer, 10 years in Corporate America and running her own business full time since 2012. She deployed twice in combat scenarios, worked with foreign governments and militaries and extensively in international business. She has an undergraduate in Criminology, an MBA and certification in Positive Psychology. She has led organizations from 3-400, loves developing people and helping them create their next steps in life and work.

She is founder of No Limits Life Empowerment Institute where she partners with professionally successful men and women to create even higher levels of success in their lifestyles and find higher levels of freedom, energy and way less BS through her Art of Living Dangerously Private Coaching program.

She is also a working glass artist, Reiki Master, Partner in Shaman Grocer (a retail store online and in Iowa City, Iowa) and Co-founder of the Midwest Reiki Festival. Her favorite time spent is doing anything soccer related or otherwise with her aspiring world cup soccer player, 10-year-old Alexander. She is a pretty big fan of gaming (PS4) with her partner Craig while solving the world's social problems.

Join Freedom Seeking Rebels in the Art of Living Dangerously Facebook Group where you can interact with others on their own paths. This is your formal invite if you dare to live dangerously.

Made in the USA
Middletown, DE
26 May 2019